W9-BZF-127

THE DARK SIDE OF A DICTATORSHIP

Measured by 1.000 years of history of the German Empire; twelve years of Nazi Dictatorship is a relative short period of time, however this era transformed Germany's position within the world – all the way up to present day times.

Over 50 million war deaths, 6 million victims in Concentration Camp's, 18 million homeless, among those that attempted escape another 3 million humans who were murdered, starved or froze to death. Innocent people had to suffer the barbaric brutalities of the Nazi regime.

CONCENTRATION CAMP'S:

Concentration camp's synonym for brutal oppression. However immediately after the take-over of power by the NSD-AP, The National Socialist Democratic Workers Party; in 1933, a number of KZ's were furnished as shelter camps by the SA (Shelter Troop); and these camps were withdrawn from normal jurisdiction; i. e. Dachau, Oranienburg (Sachsenhausen), Buchswald, Auschwitz, Flossenbürg, Theresienstadt, Treblinka etc. ... In 1939 there were many imprisoned people, more than half were criminals, the rest were Jews and Gypsies. Many nationals and foreigners were held in captivity, among those were political enemies, criminals, and antisocial persons, as well as clergymen of both confessions, members of religious sect's and Jews.

Among those held prisoner in one of the KZ's were the two sons of crown prince Franz Ferdinand and his wife (who were assassinated in 1914 in Sarajevo). They were members of the Austrian Royal Family, and Franz Ferdinand was heir to the throne (Hohenberg).

In 1942 the KZ's were also used for armament. It was not only German political prisoners that were held in the »KZ's«, but other nationalities as well; thus the camps soon became multi-national.

THE STORY OF THE »KZ'S« IS ONE OF IMMENSE SUFFERINGS:

Special Camps called »extermination camps« specialised in the »extermination of Jews«. In this battle against the Jews a special group was formed, lead by the Obersturmbannführer Adolf Eichmann, who was answerable to Himmler but acted within the guidelines of orders given by Hitler. The total extermination of the Jewish race was implemented in 1941, an extermination act that also includes Gypsies and many political undesirables – this barbaric action took the lives of millions; exactly how many – we will never really know.

How could a cultures nation of the 20th Century burden itself with such guilt? We will ask ourselves those questions for a long time to come, however, we are far from finding the right answers. We cannot undo the wrong that has happened, but we can try and stop new wrongs from taking place.

It would be a huge step towards a peaceful future if we could learn to live with and not against each other, this includes tolerance and humanity. There will never be a moral revision for the guilt, we have to live with our historical and political past and learn to accept.

Unique was the judging of the guilty in the Nürnberg trial. By committing suicide in the bunker at the Berlin Headquarters Adolf Hitler missed being put on trial. Eva Braun and the entire Goebbels family followed Hitler's example.

Because of political farsighted people and tolerance, Germany since the 2nd World War has again achieved respect and pride.

The elimination of the basic law of 1949 has re-established and guaranteed the freedom right for every citizen. Article Number One – In our constitution: **The German folk vows to acknowledge absolute Human Rights for every community to have peace and justice throughout the world.**

The tea house beneath the Berghof at the Mooslahnerkopf was named the »The Little Tea House«. Hitler liked to walk over there during his stays at the Obersalzberg. On the picture below you see both tea houses, the small one in front and the big one on top of the mountain.

Berchtesgaden
with Watzmann, 2714 m

The Kehlstein road was off limits to everyone except the Americans until it was officially re-opened

The buses are equipped with special engines and brakes to transport the visitors from Obersalzberg – Hintereck to the Eagle's Nest.

Bus terminal at Hintereck today

Buses to the Eagle's Nest in the 50's

EAGLE'S NEST

The Kehlstein was a favorite place for mountaineers and nature lovers even before the Third Reich. In the Berchtesgadener Chronical of 1791, the last Propst, Josef Conrad von Schroffenberg, appreciated the beautiful panorama from the Kehlstein. He admired the view over the Berchtesgadener Alps and into neighboring Salzburg.

With Adolf Hitler came the turning point in the history of the Obersalzberg and Kehlstein. After his first visit to the Berchtesgadener Land in 1923, Hitler was so impressed by the alpine landscape that he decided to settle on the Obersalzberg at the foot of the Kehlstein.

1933, after taking power, Hitler began to rebuild the Obersalzberg as his private residence, then later as his government headquarters.
Martin Bormann was put in charge of acquiring the land necessary for the construction. Farmers and townspeople who lived on the Obersalzberg were either forced to sell their land or it was confiscated. 670 hectars of land were also taken from the area around the Kehlstein that had been used for forestry and parkland.

1937 General inspector Ing. Fritz Todt was put in charge of constructing the road up to the Kehlstein. Under conditions that are unthinkable today, a road 6.5 kilometers long and 4 meters wide was carved out of the side of the mountains. 800 meters altitude had to be covered, five tunnels were dug out and a parking area where the buses could turn around was built at an altitude of 1700 meters. From there, there is a tunnel 3 meters high, 300 meters long straight into the mountain leading to a round hall covered in handchiseled natural stones. In the hallway is the entrance to the 124 meter high elevator shaft which was blasted out of the mountain.

The elevator has green leather seats and brass mirrors on the walls. It leads directly up into the Eagle's Nest, which was built after the road was finished.

The Eagle's Nest, an impressive granite stone building, was furnished with valuable furniture. The rooms were as follows: a huge round reception hall with many windows and a marble fireplace, dining room, kitchen, guard rooms and the pine-paneled »Scharitzkehlstube«. The road and Eagle's Nest were built in twelve monthes 1937/38 from May to October and the work had to stop at times during the winter. The cost for this technical masterpiece was 30 million Reichsmark. The structure was given to Hitler for his 50th birthday.

The Eagle's Nest was not damaged during the air raid on April 25, 1945. It was confiscated by the American occupation troops and kept under »surveillance« until 1952, although on July 18, 1952 the Eagle's Nest was retroactively re-instated as a possession of Bavaria from June 20, 1948.

After it was returned to Bavaria, the question arose whether it should be blasted off the mountain along with all the other ruins to avoid any political exhibitions. The senseless destruction of one of Germany's most beautiful look-out points or to realize the most obvious idea to turn the Eagle's Nest into a tourist attraction with positive economic results. 1952 the Bavarian Government leased the Eagle's Nest to the Berchtesgadener Chapter of the German Alpine Society. The American occupation troops had nothing against this plan. The area could finally be re-opened to the public.

The balance after 10 years management proved the decision right. The profits have been used for the renovations of the rooms, elevator, electricity, the construction of a water tank, heating system and a terrace.

After the economically positive development of Obersalzberg, the bavarian government founded the »Estate of the Berchtesgadener Land, which was at one time used for national socialist purposes, now to support charities and community projects.«

The purposes of the foundation are to support the health services, nurse the sick, education and carry on the lokal tradition.

On August 6, 1960 the foundation was officially founded with the signature of Alfons Goppel, Minister of the Interior.

The way the reputed past of the Obersalzberg-Kehlstein is given a more conventional purpose. Good management and the buses provide the foundation with funds. During the summer months thousands of visitors from around the world travel up to the Eagle's Nest with special buses. From 1734 meters above sea level they can enjoy the unsurpassable panorama and natural beauty of the Berchtesgadener Alps.

Panorama view from the Eagle's Nest over the Berchtesgadener Alps

KEHLSTEINHAUS

South side

build in 1834 m above sea level on a ledge of the Kehlstein mountain.

The Kehlsteinstraße has been constructed only for privat use at that time. Nowadays 2000 – 3000 people are carried up to the Kehlsteinhaus every day in summer.

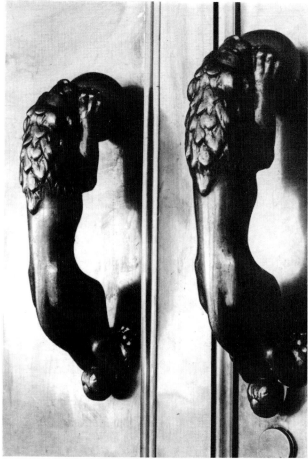

Driving up to the Kehlsteinhaus. Two bronze handles, formed like lions, were fixed to the doors of the tunnel entrance. Today key are in possession of a collector in the USA.

One of the main attractions of the Kehlstein house was and still is the big hall with its high ceiling and open marble fire place. This was a 50th birthday present to Hitler from Mussolini the 4 inch thick carpet from the emporer HIRO HITO of Japan.

The »Zirbenstube« has a large panorama window with a superb view of the Königssee, the Watzmann and the Steinernen sea.

15

The Kehlsteinhaus with its terrific view over the whole of the Berchtesgaden area is the biggest attraction in Berchtesgaden. On good summerdays some 2000 tourists come here to enjoy the view.

CONSTRUCTION OF THE KEHLSTEIN-ROAD

under the direction of Ing. Fritz Todt

Ing. FRITZ TODT, born Sept. 9, 1891 in Pforzheim.

1922 member of NSDAP. 1933 General inspector for German road maintenance, in charge of the construction of the Autobahn. In 1938 he founded the Todt Organisation and also built the west wall along the Rhine river.

1940 Reichsminister for weapons and ammunition, 1941 Reichsminister for water and energy. 1942 Todt died in an airplane crash near Rastenburg.

Ing. Fritz Todt (left) with newsreel reporter, Anton Hafner

The Kehlstein road today

Documentary photo series
from Anton Hafner
ordered by General inspector Ing. Fritz Todt

17

Surveying in the mountainous terrain was extremely difficult for the survey engineers.

In the beginning of 1938 the General inspector for road maintenance, Dipl.-Ing. Fritz Todt, was given the order to build the road up to the Eagle's Nest. The Road was to be finished for Hitler's 50th birthday, April 20, 1939.

Martin Bormann, who initiated the project, planned it as a gigantic surprise for Hitler's birthday.

An unbelievable short period for such an enormously difficult plan. They could not begin immediately. First that terrain possibilities were studied, usually under the worst weather conditions. Snow drifts, loose rocks, danger of avalanches and freezing conditions prevented much of the work from starting. The fact that the entire project was completed on time is due to the ambition and zeal of the technicians, engineers and laborers. It is impossible to even think of undertaking such a project today when one remembers the limited tools and simple machinery available at that time.

*Even as winter
begins the preparations
continue*

In the beginning, machinery, tools and supplies were carried up by the men on their shoulders

Lodging for the workers under an overhanging rock

As the work advances it is made easier with cables, pulleys, and hoists to transport the stone and other materials on and off the steeper parts of the mountain

*Stone walls, known as cyclop walls, are often used to protect
the roads from rock- and landslides*

Chipping away all the loose rocks to avoid falling rocks.
Along the more dangerous stretches retaining walls were constructed
to protect the road from landslides and rocks

Transporting the tools and material with a hoist

With great difficulty the terrace for the road was carved out of the mountain one meter at a time

*Complete tracks
were set up
to mix the
cement needed*

Bus ride up to Eagle's Nest

Bus ride up to Eagle's Nest

Approximately 3000 men worked on this project. Mostly Italian stone masons worked with hammer and chisel to form the rocks to be used to build the bridges and retaining walls.

Work was done in shifts around the clock. The area was floodlit at night so work could continue in the dark as well. Kitchen and sleeping quarters were set up on rock piles and under hanging cliffs. The laborers worked under the most difficult and dangerous conditions.

Martin Bormann, the creator of the Obersalzberg, was obsessed with finishing the project on time. He spured workers on to work harder and faster. Unexpected technical problems were solved almost immediately by Ing. Fritz Todt and his team.

Martin Bormann considered this project not only as representing the »Third Reich«, but as the symbol for the beginning of a new era in the field of construction.

With stone drills the blasting holes were bored and the rocks were removed

The simpliest tools were used to work the stones. Explosives were used to break down the rocks to smaller, usable material

29

The rock dug out of the tunnel was used to fill terraces of the road.
This saved time because the material did not need to be transported down the mountain.

It was not always possible to build the road along the mountain on terraces. Five tunnels had to be blasted out of the limestone then the walls had to be lined with cement to keep to porous rock from falling.

The amount of labor and funds invested in this project seem meager when compared to the rest of the construction done during this era.

All of Germany experienced a boom in the construction sector. Highways, apartment houses, government buildings, public facilities, a dense network of railroad tracks, airport and other structures were begun.

Adolf Hitler did not personally take part in planning or building anything on the Obersalzberg or Kehlstein.

Blasting a tunnel

A stonemason works on the natural stone by hand. In the background the Königssee, Watzmann and Sea of Stone range

Stone drills are used to cut the rocks down along the upper part of the Kehlstein road

The larger stones are broken down to usable size

Stone mason at work

Feverishly working, a race against time. That this project could be organized in such a short time seemed reasonable, but that it could actually be realized showed the ambition and determination of the engineers and laborers.

The highest performance was demanded but the workers were given high wages and were guaranteed employment and social services.

The Eagle's Nest and the road were completed in time to be given over their determined purpose for Hitler's 50th birthday.

The project was not erected for any material reason, but to realize an idea. Today the building is used as if it had been built for just such an economic purpose.

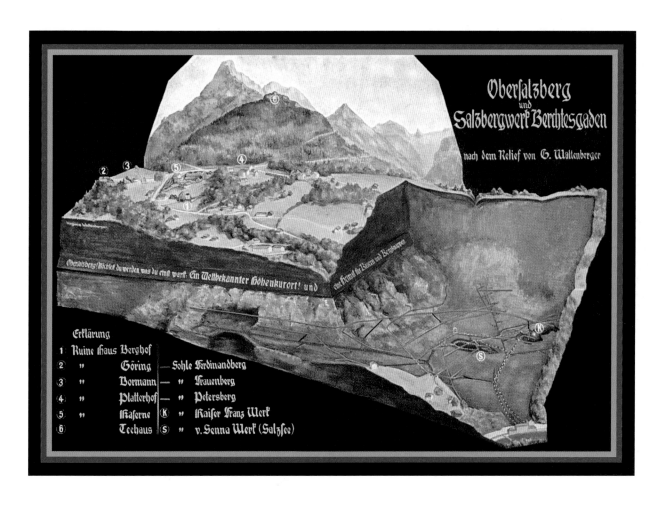

Oberfalzberg
und
Salzbergwerk Berchtesgaden

nach dem Relief von G. Wattenberger

Oberfalzberg! Blicke du werden, was du einst warst: Ein Weltbekannter Höhenkurort! und ein Freund für Bauer und Bergknappe

Erklärung

1 Ruine Haus Berghof
2 „ Göring — Sohle Ferdinandberg
3 „ Bormann — „ Frauenberg
4 „ Platterhof — „ Petersberg
5 „ Kaserne (K) „ Kaiser Franz Werk
6 „ Teehaus (S) „ v. Senna Werk (Salzfee)

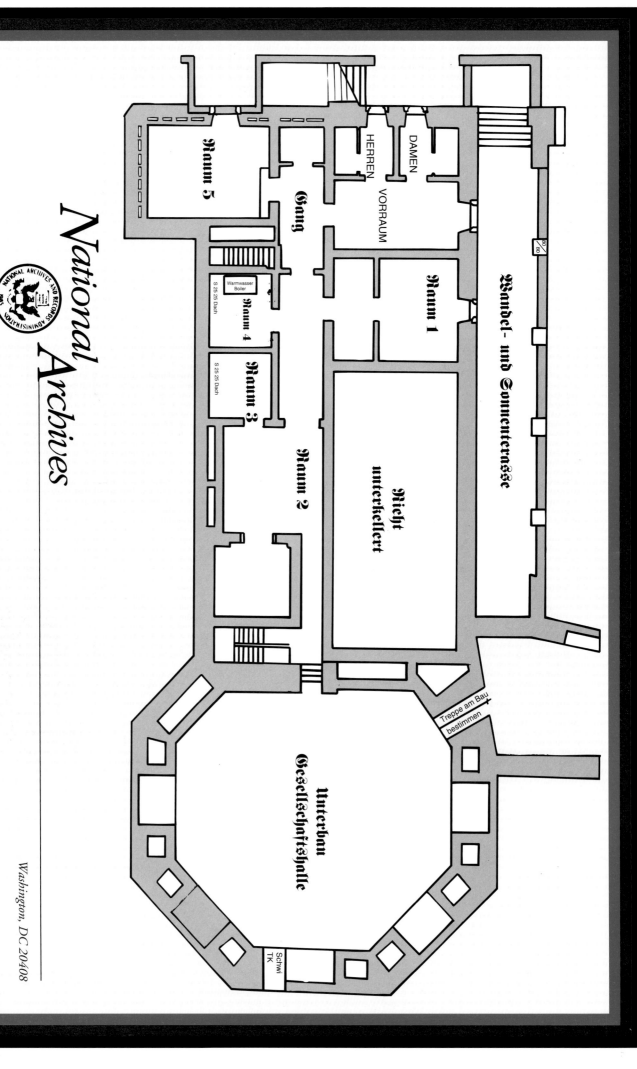

National Archives

Washington, DC 20408

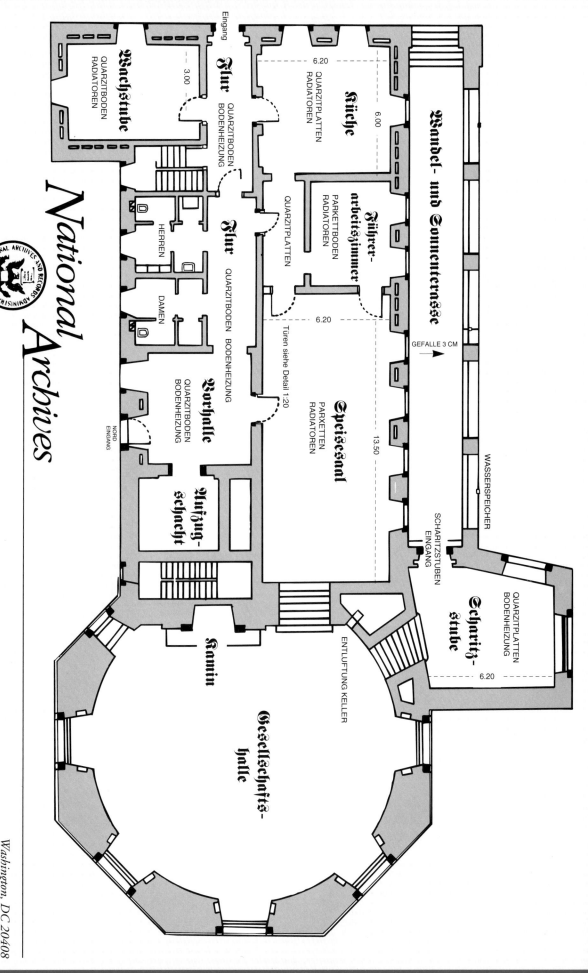

National Archives

Washington, DC 20408

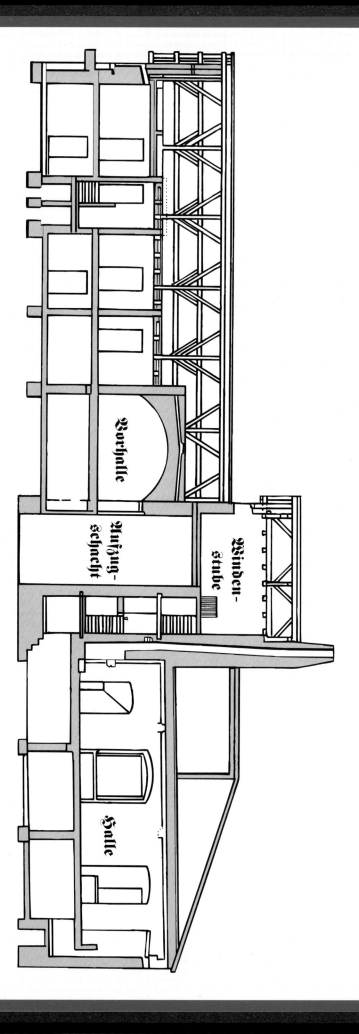

National Archives

Washington, DC 20408

PARKING AREA KEHLSTEIN

Once one has reached the parking area there are two possibilities to reach the Eagle's Nest. One can either use the elevator or else cover the last 124 meters on foot. The well organized bus system sees to it that all guests are easily transported back and forth. As they are needed, up to the parking area Kehlstein. The points where the buses can pass is set up by CB radio. When the weather is clear the trip up to the Eagle's Nest in an unforgettable event for every visitor. For security rea- sons the buses can only run form mid-May til the end of October. It would be very difficult as well as expensive to clear the snow off the road. Ava- lanches and falling rocks would make such a pro- ject close to impossible.

Entrance to the tunnel on the parking area Kehlstein. The plateau is large enough for the buses to turn around and for the guests to board.

THE FOOTPATH

As an alternative to the bus there is a footpath up to the Eagle's Nest. A footpath branches off the road and winds its way, partially through the forest, up the steep high alpine terrain. The hiker is presented with a splendid view of the surrounding mountains.

Behind the Rossfeld mountain, which is opposite, the city of Salzburg is located. On clear, sunny days it is possible to see across into neighboring Austria.

Rare alpine flowers and grasses, some of which are protected, line the path. The beauty only nature can offer is reward enough for the strenuous ascent.

The Elevator

A tunnel of Untersberg marble leads to an impressive round hall. From here the visitor is brought directly into the Eagle's Nest in a luxurious elevator.

Round hall with elevator door

Tunnel

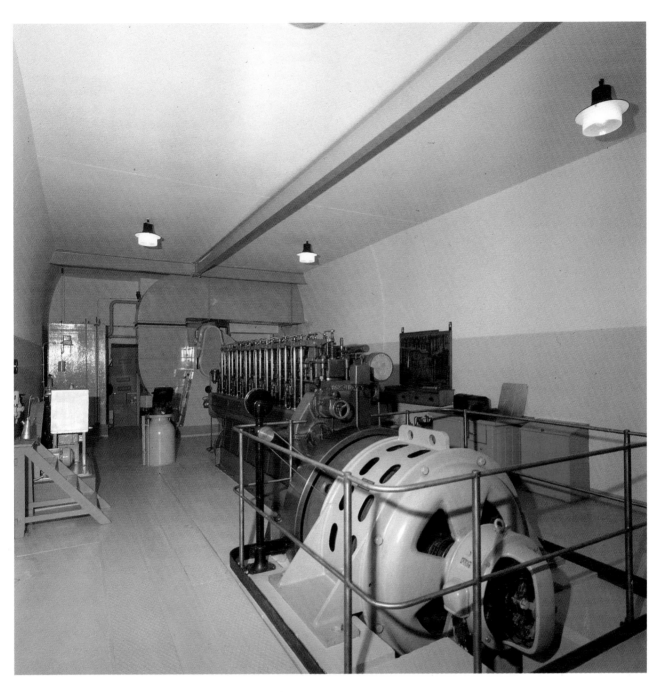

In a separate engine room there is an emergency generator run by an U-boat diesel engine which is still used today to supply the Eagle's Nest with electricity during a blackout.

Next to the tunnel is a separate shaft for the cables and heating pipes.

A cable tunnel runs parallel to the main tunnel and ends in a big cavern deep in the mountain in which stands an U-boat diesel motor which automatically provided emergency power in the event of an electrical failure.

The lift shaft

THE DINING ROOM – THEN AND NOW

As you can see in the photo above, there have been no changes made in this room. Only the furniture has been renewed. The wall-paneling and the cassette ceiling are part of the original interior.

Below: Dining room today
Above: Dining room before 1945

The Conference Hall today

*A picture of the marble fireplace –
a present from the Duce – Mussolini*

The construction as well as the interior of the room is adapted to the surroundings. The natural stone walls are in a half-circle and the wooden ceiling softens the atmosphere of the room. The front windows open the view to the magnificent panorama of the mountains and valleys. On clear days the viewer can see into parts of Austria as well.

The open fireplace was a birthday present for Hitler's 50th birthday from Mussolini. The more valuable decorative objects disappeared into private possession during the occupation. To the right next to the fireplace a wide staircase leads up to the dining room.

AFTER 1945

*Conference room in the Eagle's Nest,
American soldiers in the conference or reception hall
after the war*

*General Eisenhower's visit
at the Eagle's Nest
in early Summer 1945.*

Back to the terrace that is around the back of the Eagle's Nest.

Tables and chairs invite visitors to relax in the middle of the fascinating world around them and enjoy a meal. A narrow path leads up to the cross at the peak. On some days one can observe nature at play. Within minutes the curtain of fog can lift to reveal the massive peaks in the background. An impressive event one has to witness to understand.

THE WAY DOWN

Impressed and content the visitors begin the journey back down the valley. After having a last look at the panorama of the mountains surrounding them, they board the buses which are waiting to take them down. Contented looks on their faces are living proof that it was a successful excursion. Many of the guests, whether from Germany or foreign countries, return again and again to the Eagle's Nest. The Berchtesgadener Land is often a favorite place to enjoy the beauty of nature in the Alps.

The adventurous bus ride along the steep rock walls and deep gorges takes about 20 minutes. Just a few more turns and few you're back at the terminal at Hintereck.

In the shops there is time for a few more souvenirs, postcards or alpine clothing or a stop in the café to quench your thirst.

Those visitors who did not come by automobile can take the service buses down to the village of Berchtesgaden.

MERCEDES BENZ OF ADOLF HITLER

This Mercedes, Typ 770, was a special construction for Adolf Hitler:
Weight: 4780 kg
Tires: 400 CV
Bumpers: 13 cm
PS: 250
Speed: 200 km/h
Windows: 43 mm thick bullet-proof glass
Tank: 300 l fuel
Cooler: 18 mm thick
Running boards: 13 cm

Adolf Hitler
and Eva Braun
leaving the automobile

The automobile was exhibited in an Auto museum in Lyon, France, in March 1982. Research shows that the car was taken to the United States to be displayed by American soldiers after the war. The car disappeared for a long period of time and reappeared at an auction. Today the car can be seen at exhibitions.

BERCHTESGADEN

The constant presence of Hitler and other party members on the Obersalzberg changed the way of life in the romantic Berchtesgadener Land. The quiet, relaxing atmosphere in the small village on the edge of the Bavarian Alps had been used for catering to the Bavarian royal family, clerical nobility and industrialists. This atmosphere was ruined by uniformed SA troops and the hordes of people who came to hear Hitler's speeches.

The economical situation undoubtedly made it easier for Adolf Hitler to obtain support. Everyone was willing to believe the propaganda promising a new and better future. Thus Hitler and his political associates could gain power that would lead them to a national catastrophe 12 years later.

Speaking at Breitwies, Berchtesgaden. People came from all over Germany and Austria to hear Hitler's speeches.

SA troops at the village fountain in Berchtesgaden.

FORMER OBERSALZBERG AREA

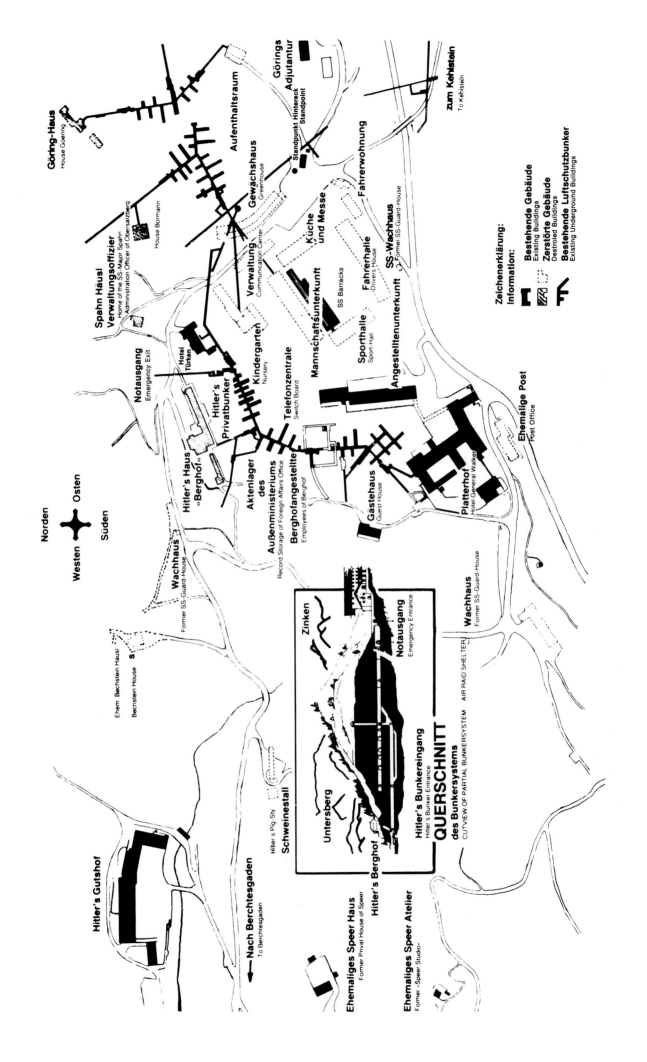

Norden
Westen — **Osten**
Süden

Göring-Haus
House Goering

Görings Adjarntur

zum Kehlstein
To Kehlstein

Aufenthaltsraum

Standpunkt Hintereck Standpoint

Gewächshaus
Greenhouse

Spahn Häusl Verwaltungsoffizier
Home of the SS-Major Spahn
Administration Officer of Obersalzberg

House Bormann

Küche und Messe

Fahrerwohnung

Verwaltung
Communication Center

SS-Wachhaus
Former SS-Guard-House

Mannschaftsunterkunft
SS Barracks

Fahrerhalle
Drivers House

Notausgang
Emergency Exit

Hotel Türken

Kindergarten
Nursery

Sporthalle
Sport-Hall

Hitler's Haus »Berghof«

Hitler's Privatbunker

Telefonzentrale
Switch Board

Angestelltenunterkunft

Wachhaus
Former SS-Guard-House

Aktenlager des Außenministeriums
Record Storage of Foreign Affairs Office

Berghofangestellte
Employees of Berghof

Gästehaus
Guest House

Platterhof
Hotel General Walker

Ehemalige Post
Post Office

Hitler's Gutshof

Nach Berchtesgaden
To Berchtesgaden

Ehem. Bechstein Häusl
Bechstein House

Hitler's Pig-Sty
Hitler's Pig-Sty

Schweinestall

Ehemaliges Speer Haus
Former Privat House of Speer

Hitler's Berghof

Ehemaliges Speer Atelier
Former »Speer Studio«

Untersberg

Zinken

Notausgang
Emergency Entrance

Hitler's Bunkereingang
Hitler's Bunker Entrance

QUERSCHNITT des Bunkersystems
CUT VIEW OF PARTIAL BUNKERSYSTEM   AIR RAID SHELTER

Wachhaus
Former SS-Guard-House

Zeichenerklärung: Information:

Bestehende Gebäude
Existing Buildings

Zerstörte Gebäude
Destroied Buildings

Bestehende Luftschutzbunker
Existing Underground Buildings

55

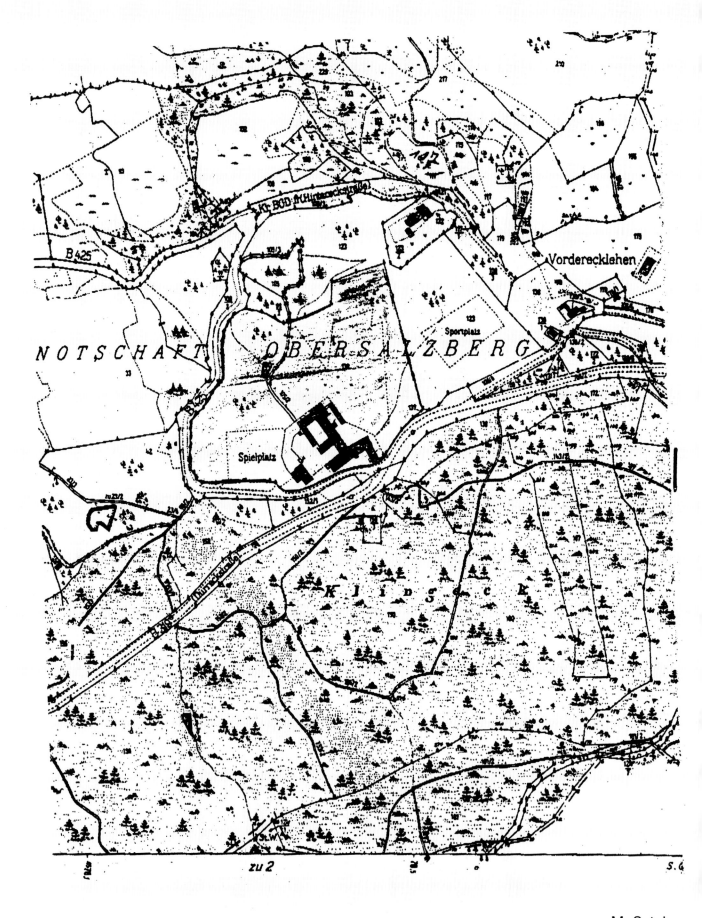

Maßstab

Landesvermessungsamt München 1854

31.38.52.64.77

56

OBERSALZBERG, HOTEL »PENSION MORITZ«

Hotel »Pension Moritz«, to the left a guest house used for high political leaders and military officials during the NS era.

*The poet
and writer
Richard Voss.*

PLATTERHOF

Pension Moritz, later renamed the Platterhof and known from the novel »Zwei Menschen« by Richard Voss, was a favorite attraction for prominent guests even before Hitler.

During the twenties, Hitler enjoyed the Obersalzberg and was often a guest at the Platterhof. Later, when Hitler bought the „Wachenfeld« the NSDAP bought the Platterhof and remodeled it for guests of the party.

The Platterhof was damaged during the air raid at the end of the war. After the war it was rebuilt and now serves the American army for rest and recreation.

*A monument in honor
of Richard Voss
was placed above
the Pension Moritz.*

57

*The old Platterhof,
on the right is the
Bodner farm.*

*The Hotel »Türken«
was an inn for mountaineers
and alpine society members before
Hitler's era.*

*Memorial on the
Göring hill,
a sign of the powerfull
inhabitants
of the Obersalzberg.*

Above: The employees house with the Watzmann and Hochkalter mountains in the background.

DER PLATTERHOF after its rebuild in 1941. Today it looks almost the same except for the shop and post office in the foreground which do not exist anymore. The employees house was ruined but has been made into a single store garage. The hotel was named after Judith Platter, it was a luxury hotel with 150 beds and was open to all.

Except for the Platterhof hotel, which could be reached by the way of Oberau, the whole Obersalzberg was off limits to the public. All the other ways in were closed and guarded around the clock. The two pictures show the guest house Hoher Göll.

*The Platterhof
after the air raid.
In the foreground
the SS Barracks,
the Kindergarten and
model museum.*

*The Platterhof today.
Hotel General Walker*

*The Guest house
below the Platterhof.*

*Between the Platterhof
and the bus terminal
at Hintereck today stood the guard house.*

Winter scenery at the Obersalzberg. The mountain in the background of the Berghof is the Reiteralpe.

Residential home and studio of architect Albert Speer.

THE BERGHOF

Soon after Hitler's take-over, the Obersalzberg became the second headquarters. After a number of renovations the Berghof was transformed into a mountain retreat for private as well as public services. Besides the private rooms for Hitler and Eva Braun, there was a dining room, living room, kitchen, offices for Hitler and his aides, private guestrooms and of course the most impressive room, the conference hall. It was furnished with valuable paintings, carpets, gobelins and refined pieces of furniture. An italian marble fireplace and a huge, sinkable picture window, which was sunk by an electric motor, completed the interior decoration of the unique room.

Above:
The Berghof after
all the renovations

The conference hall

The Berghof after
the air raid.

The Berghof was destroyed twice. Partially damaged first on April 25, 1945 by the British Royal Air Force. Then on May 4, 1945, the remaining SS troops set it on fire.

The Berghof today. It has been reconstructet several times.

The guest house Hoher Göll. Part of this house was used as an office by Martin Bormann but its main role was as a guest house for visitors to Bormann.

Görings house, at the edge of the forest, with a superb view to the famous Untersberg mountains (borderland of Austria), was situated on a hill named »Göringshügel«.

Seat on top of the »Göringshügel«. The table is made of Ziller-Marmor.

The Göring house after the air raid.
In 1952 the Freestate of Bavaria ordered all ruins
to be cleared off the mountain.

GÖRING-HOUSE ON OBERSALZBERG

REICHSMARSCHALL HERMANN GÖRING

*Living room
in Göring's house.*

BORMANN HOUSE

Martin Bormann

MARTIN BORMANN, head of the NS party, was born in Halberstadt on January 16, 1900. Hitler put him charge of his private fortune and also of the necessary constructions of the Obersalzberg and Berghof. Later he was granted total rule over the Obersalzberg. He advanced to »Reichsleiter« (Leader of the Reich) and had the authority of a chancellor. During the Nürnberger Trials Bormann, who was supposedly still alive after the war, was sentenced, in absentee, to death. Only in 1973 was Bormann officially pronounced dead by the State Prosecuter in Frankfurt.

The Bormann house stood just opposite the Berghof and was completely destroyed. On the right in the photo the Bormann house with the Berghof and Türken (SS) in the background.

East wing of the barrack complex.

THE »SS«-BARRACKS

Quarters and drill yards for the permanent contingent of guards on the Obersalzberg.

Shooting practice in underground shooting galeries was part of the daily exercises as well as fitness training in the court yard.

*Main entrance
to the barracks after
the bombing*

HOTEL »ZUM TÜRKEN«

The Bavaria government ruled that under no circumstances what so ever should anyone be allowed to re-settle on the Obersalzberg. Especially no one who had been affiliated with the Nazi party.

One exception was made, Theresa Partner was allowed to buy back the badly damaged Gasthof »Zum Türken«, which had been owned and run by her father, Karl Schuster. In 1933 Karl Schuster had been forced by the SA to sell his house and business.

»Der Türken« was the SS headquarters during the Nazi era. The fog unit was also stationed there. The fog unit was responsible for the camouflage in case of air raids. The Obersalzberg was covered with a cloud of fog.

In 1949 Theresa Partner began to rebuild the »Zum Türken«. She soon succeeded in building an alpine resort hotel which offers a splendid panorama of the surroundings. Her daughter, Ingrid Scharfenberg, carries on this tradition with her family as well. In the »Zum Türken« is the only official entrance to the bunker, still open to the public, which was directly connected with the Berghof. A small bit left out of the historical past of the »Türken«.

Crowds of people waited each day along the road below the »Türken« for a glimpse of Adolf Hitler

THE BUNKER SYSTEMS OF OBERSALZBERG

In 1943, the question of security and protection in the case of an air raid arose. Despite Dr. Goebbels propaganda promising a sure victory, one could not overlook the fact that the fall of the 3rd. Reich was at hand.

German cities were under constant attack from the American and British air forces. Thousands were dying in these attacks.

Under top secret conditions plans were drawn up for an underground bunker system. Under the direction of German engineers, Italian and Czechoslovakian workers started construction of the air raid shelters. The simple plans for an air raid shelter soon turned out to be an underground fortress with all the technical know-how available at the time.

A highly technical system controlled the sewage, ventilation, heating and electricity.

About 2.800 meters of tunnels connected approximately 80 rooms. Some were functionally equipped and others were luxuriously furnished.

Entrance to the bunkers at Hotel Türken.

Iron door-way to the kennels for Hitler's watch-dogs.

The use of the bunkers were set up as follows:

Wood-paneled, richly carpeted, and exclusively furnished rooms, baths and kitchens were reserved for the personal use by Hitler, Bormann and Göring, and could be found below their homes.

73

The rest of the bunkers were used as work rooms, living quarters, engine rooms and store rooms for the statt and personel. There was even a room for Hitler's german shepard dogs with a separate entrance.

Heavy iron doors and openings for machine guns were installed to ward off the first attacks.

Clothing, important documents and food supplies were kept in the private bunkers for Hitler, Bormann and Göring.

Items that could no longer be stored in the secret sections of the bunkers toward the end of the war were either plundered or fell into the hands of the occupation troops.

Left: Machine gun rooms with openings to shoot through and also see through. Right: After the war American soldiers tried to shoot through a wall of the bunker with a bazooka.

Switchboard in the Türken Hotel – the headquarters for the SS (secret police)

74

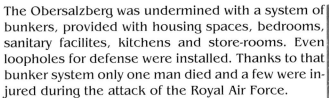

The Obersalzberg was undermined with a system of bunkers, provided with housing spaces, bedrooms, sanitary facilites, kitchens and store-rooms. Even loopholes for defense were installed. Thanks to that bunker system only one man died and a few were injured during the attack of the Royal Air Force.

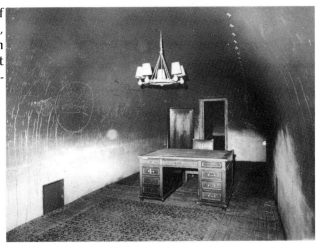

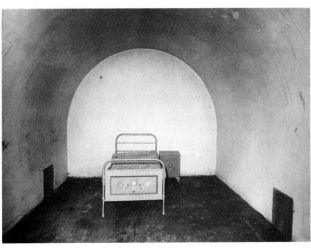

BOMBING OF THE OBERSALZBERG
BY THE RAF ON APRIL 25, 1945

MAY 4, 1945 END OF THE NS-ERA ON THE OBERSALZBERG

Assuming to find government officials and SS battle troops on the Obersalzberg, American and French Divisions were sent to take Berchtesgaden and the supposedly »Alpine Fortress«. The American 101st Airborne Division was able to occupy Berchtesgaden before the French.

Berchtesgaden surrendered without resistance to the Allies. The Obersalzberg was also taken without a battle.

American tanks rolling onto the Schloßplatz in Berchtesgaden

On May 5th Mayor Sandrock and Governor Jakob officially turned the village of Berchtesgaden over to the Americans and the area became part of American Zone.

American soldiers in the large picture window of the Berghof on the Obersalzberg

With plans to destroy the buildings once used by the NSDAP, Prime Minister Högner came to the Obersalzberg accompanied by a delegation. He was driven in vehicles from the American occupation troops.

Thanks to influential intervention by open-minded advisors, the Kehlsteinhaus was left intact.

The final decision was made and, with only a few exceptions, all of the ruins on the Obersalzberg were destroyed.

On April 30, 1952 the work began. The buildings that had been built during the Third Reich could only be torn down with help of explosives.

The mountain farm after the bombardement. A strange formation arose by soot and fire in form of a »shape of death«. Pretty correct. The fotograph below shows on the right the farm and in the front the demolished »Spahn Häusel« named to the leader of administration SS Sturmbannführer Spahn.

The ruin of Hitlers house with the famous window.

Visitors liked to write their names on the black walls and liked to rest on the steps of the Berghof.

ACHTUNG!
AB HIER SPERRGEBIET!
ALLEN ZIVILFAHRZEUGEN SOWIE
ZIVILPERSONEN IST DAS BEFAHREN
BZW. BETRETEN DES OBERSALZBERGES
OHNE SCHRIFTLICHE GENEHMIGUNG
VOM SECURITY OFFICE BERCHTESGADEN
VERBOTEN.

After the occupation by the Americans the Obersalzberg was off limits to the Germans.

The Berghof, empty, burned and plundered.

The post office, followers' house and business building were totally destroyed by the bombing attack. The Platterhof hotel showed only unimportant damage. After repair the Platterhof was confiscated by the US occupying power and was used as a resort for army members.
Below: The Bormannhaus was totally destroyed by the bombardement.

Görings house was destroyed by bombing also in front of the house. In 1952 the ruins were blown up by order of the bavaria government.

Totally destroyed was also the area of the barracks. Only a few pillars remind to the former drill-ground and the soldiers on guard. The greenhouse, gardening, driver's house and the hall for the official vehicles were also considerable damaged.

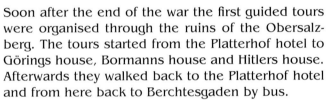

Soon after the end of the war the first guided tours were organised through the ruins of the Obersalzberg. The tours started from the Platterhof hotel to Görings house, Bormanns house and Hitlers house. Afterwards they walked back to the Platterhof hotel and from here back to Berchtesgaden by bus.

In 1952 all ruins were removed by order of the Bavarian Government. Nothing should remain to people of the war and the disaster afterwards.

The Gardening at the Obersalzberg was bombed and totally destroyed.

Plunderer at the Obersalzberg.